LIFE OUTTA LOCKDOWN

2021

BEYOND CLOSED DOORS

Dee Bailey

Life Outta Lockdown
Beyond Closed Doors

Authored by Lead Author Dee Bailey
©copyright Simply Deez Events 2021
Cover art work & design Marcia M Publishing House

Edited by Marcia M Publishing House Editorial Team Published by Marcia M Spence of Marcia M Publishing House, West Bromwich, West Midlands the UNITED KINGDOM B71

MARCIA M
PUBLISHING HOUSE

www.marciampublishing.com

Table of Contents

Foreword

The pandemic was a leveller for everyone. Families and friends were lost and lifelong friendships found.

I met the Life Inna Lockdown women when I was approached by Dee to say a few words of inspiration to the women on a Zoom chat. However, they turned out to be my salvation. I instantly felt an affinity with all the women; all their characters shone through: the quiet, outspoken, quirky and gregarious.

What we all had in common was the trepidation we felt in the face of uncharted waters.

I instantly gained a hole heap of sisters and was enveloped in love. We had an unspoken understanding that we would all go forward to together or perish alone.

That first meeting, I was to speak for ten minutes. Quite a few hours later I was still there, glued to the screen. I may have been a Lord Mayor, the woman who had it all together! But my fear and vulnerability were as raw as the women on that Zoom.

They were my inspiration and pulled me through what would be one of the most testing periods of my life.

I love and respect each and every one of these amazing women and have forged a lifelong friendship with them.

Thank you for sharing your valuable time with me.

Councillor Anna Rothery, former Lord Mayor of Liverpool.

Acknowledgements

Firstly, we would like to send our love to all those who have lost friends and loved ones over these past 18 months. For us, the survivors, this book will always be a reminder of how amazing we can be when we support one another.

Thank you...

The co-authors thank all their families and friends in the UK and overseas who have been with us on this journey.

Total Wellbeing Luton, who part-funded this project. Simply Deez Events CIC sponsor and to organisations who have supported such as Bedfordshire Recovery College, Near Neighbours and the Mayor of Houghton Regis Clare Copleston.

Marcia M Spence and her team at the Publishing House for your continued support through this whole process.

A very special thanks to Councillor Anna Rothery, former Lord Mayor of Liverpool, for constantly championing us at Simply Deez Events, the work we do and being our number one supporter!

The Life Outta Lockdown Crew

Aug 2021

Introduction

My name is Dee Bailey, Founder/CEO of Simply Deez Events CIC. The Life Inna Lockdown Zooms began (and continue to this day) back in April 2020. Veronica Ebanks suggested we needed to document these unprecedented times. So, last year *Life Inna Lockdown 2020: Behind Closed Doors* was published. Currently, over 800 books worldwide have been sold!

Friends and family have been asking when is it coming? I am so proud to announce the sequel!

This book features some new co-authors; friends we have met along our lockdown journey.

How was it for you, June 20 – August 21? Life has been a roller coaster for all of us. In this book each of the authors shares their own personal journey with you.

Stories to give you hope, strength and words of encouragement. You are not alone.

Chapter 1.
I Found the Courage
Ronald Amanze

I am testing myself beyond my expectations
Unsure if this makes sense
It's chaotic but it's my normal
Showing a different side of me, allowing my creative
spirit to roam free, finally stepping out in courage
and sharing emotional vulnerability.

Unsure if I am doing the right thing,
Unresolved conflict and turmoil within,
At times I get exhausted and feel like giving in.
While something abstract and unreal
Stimulates the neurons in my brain.

Trying to bypass anxiety and stress
Invariably I seem to gravitate to love songs,
frequencies, and romantic creativity.

As life continues to embarrass and intrigue me
I focus on time-shifting melodies and memories,

Cutting round corners running from the feds,
Ducking down alleyways laughing off our heads,
Jumping over fences and into garden sheds.
Those juvenile days are memories I will never shed.

Still with optimism in all the right places
Enthusiasm in all the right spaces
Now I just need to survive
The changes lurking in my brain,
The dementia diagnosis and the climate change of
my brain,
My impulsive nature and from the things I must
refrain.

This is remarkable
Searching for a missing part of me
Now every time I pass a window
I peep in to see if I can find me.

Anyway, I am not owning this
As unsure if this makes sense.
At times I am misunderstood,
But today is the truth of me and I will own it anyway,
Because all I can be is me, being courageous and
creative, that's me.
As everyone loves a box of smiles.

Ronald Amanze ©

Ronald Amanze

I'm sharing a piece of me. There's so much inside of me that now needs creativity. Well, what can I say, as someone living with a brain injury and after I was diagnosed with onset of dementia? I was very confused, sad and in denial. But I was also determined to keep living a meaningful life. It was difficult at times because there were people who didn't understand me because of my health condition, and I found myself being stigmatised and excluded from mainstream services. Often, I felt culturally misunderstood. Every day now I feel full of enthusiasm and the joy of life; there's so much I now appreciate and value which I didn't notice before. It can be so sad yet so beautiful how a life-changing diagnosis can wake you up to new realities.

Chapter 2.
It Is Not the End.
It Is the Beginning
Jo Maddix

It's June 2020. I had hoped that a cure would have been found and the virus blasted out of existence, leaving a cleaner environment, quiet streets and the new normal being the majority of us working from home – a healthier and happier world. Utopia.

I was wrong and the pandemic continues. The terms COVID, lockdown, unprecedented, and the R number are indelibly lodged in our vocabulary. The UK is in its second wave and the desperate race to find a vaccine continues. The scientists, politicians, doctors, social media stars and so-called experts are jumping excitedly in their seats with their hands raised wanting to be picked because they think they have the right answers to the six-million-dollar question.

There was a reprieve at Christmas, which turned out to have been a mistake, and we returned to lockdown.

Social distancing, jobs lost, companies closing down, some being furloughed by the government. Missed education, curtailed celebration of marriages and births, limited travel, no holidays, and more deaths. The new year welcomes more of the same but begins to divide the public on whether to take the new vaccine when it comes, or to exercise our democratic right to choose what goes into our bodies.

People are emerging from their homes into back gardens, from isolation, relearning social cues, social awkwardness, not knowing whether to offer a hug or an elbow. Questioning eyes are peering out of faces suspiciously wondering if this person or that person will be the reason for their demise. Faces have disappeared under masked coverings, robbing us of our identity. Mouths silenced but minds muddled and screaming, asking to be let out of this nightmare, this world of uncertainty with loss of control and fear.

I put my hand over my ears to block out the noise of COVID. I try to sleep but my mind's eye exposes me to terrible nightmares. Sometimes I am being prodded and poked by instruments being stuck up my nose and down my throat, syringes full of poison turning me into a mutant, and I join a nation of zombies, giving in to mind control, and finally anarchy.

Sometimes something sharp is piercing my upper arm and a rush of anxiety travels through my veins, not knowing whether it has been sent to help or hinder my fight to stay alive. I break out into a cold sweat, my head is pounding, I am exhausted, and my body is aching. I can't breathe. I watch doctors and nurses rushing around me as I lie in a hospital bed on a ventilator. I drift into unconsciousness and I feel a sense of peace come over me. I am brought back to reality and the still small voice of my subconscious says, 'Wake up; you are having a bad dream.'

I open my eyes and nothing of importance has changed and I begin to experience mental fatigue from the constant dialogue around COVID. Unable to escape it, I try to switch off, only to find that there is something else emerging from the cobwebs of my brain. I am taken to a place which feels mildly familiar but also foreign.

Slowing my mind, I see the image of a woman intensely staring back at me. She is alone. Her eyes are unseeing. Her lips form words which escape me. I sense her presence, but she is absent. I can feel her but cannot touch her. I know she exists; she is daughter, wife, mother, sister, but she is not herself. In the quiet of lockdown with no other place to go but inwards, I realise I am starting a journey of self-discovery. I have been drifting through life accepting my role as carer, nurturer, provider, worker, fetching, carrying, doing, and being done to.

It's August 2021. The vaccine programme has been rolled out. Fewer people in hospital. New variants surfacing and transmitting the poisonous virus even quicker than before. In some way we are still prisoners to COVID, restricted to where we can go without conditions which take away choice. Research is still continuing with no conclusive answers to the virus, which keeps us afraid for ourselves and our families. The worry is causing a rise in mental health problems. It's been a challenge not having any control of the future and, in many respects, I am being held hostage by the virus, which selfishly insists on being a part of my decisions.

So, has anything changed, I ask myself? Maybe not with the pandemic, but I have made the decision not to be consumed by it. I am learning to be present, letting go of the reins and slowing down, remembering what I did yesterday, having a new relationship with the person that I am, releasing the pressure and stressors of living which I have created. Knowing that I have the power to just stop, and the world will keep turning. Looking outside of myself and seeing with new eyes the people in my life from which I have been absent while lending myself to the version of life that says, 'I am too busy, I don't have time, I can't, I have to do this, I have to do that.' Realising that I have a lot to be thankful for: I have a roof over my head, food to eat, employment, love, friends, family. I have my health and the power to choose. This is my new normal.

I am getting reacquainted with myself, feeling a sense of renewed energy and thinking of new possibilities. Understanding that the feeling in the pit of my stomach can be my instincts and I should listen to it. Being self-aware and stepping outside my island and just being. No longer afraid to be wrong but learning from every experience. Knowing that in order to help others, I have to start with myself. Knowing that life is fragile and short. I say, 'It is not the end. It is the beginning.'

Jo Maddix

Jo grew up in London and has a background in health and social care management. She is currently working in a specialist role as a mental health professional. She also works as a practice educator and mentor to pre-qualified and practising social workers. She loves to read and has always lost herself in books since she was a child.

In her spare time, she does voluntary work for a local charity. She likes travelling, going to the theatre, and running. She has completed several half-marathons and one marathon.

Becoming a co-author has taken her on a journey of soul-searching which continues to produce new discoveries of self and life. Her contribution to *Life Inna Lockdown 2020* and now the second volume is giving her confidence to venture outside her comfort zone and do new things. She is edging ever closer to trying her hand at writing her first book.

Chapter 3.
A Reflection of Time
Sandra Moore

Healing, surviving and thriving has been my mantra since I last shared my *Life Inna Lockdown* story. Like it or not, we now have a health and mental well-being pandemic.

I wanted to help those that needed a safe space to connect with themselves and others, so I launched my health and well-being practice in September 2020, delivering breath work and meditation sessions weekly; this has been a delicious, nourishing and nurturing journey.

My personal practice of meditation, breath work and qigong really supported my mental health and well-being and I can truly say I am thriving. However, there were days I felt angry, irritable and downright fed up with the mixed messages from the government, the negativity, bullying, blackmail, bias and deceptive reporting by the media. I stopped reading and listening to the news as it was full of doom and gloom.

My work life became very busy in September 2020, looking after existing clients as well as working on new projects that not only provided new challenges, but also gave me the opportunity to be working in the hub of the pandemic with two regional public health teams. If you remember, I had a mixture of emotions about the first lockdown. I was happy about gaining more free time but concerned about my income. On reflection, even though I have been busy, I still had more free time.

How I chose to use this was, and still is, totally up to me. Self-organisation is key. Some of you will know this as 'time management'; there is that word, 'time', again. As I am writing this, procrastination waves and says, "Remember me? How many movies and Netflix series did you watch?" Waving back, I answered, "I am not going to feel guilty about chilling and taking time for me." Procrastination shakes her head, rolls her eyes and disappears.

Seriously though, when I reflect on this time, I realise that resilience runs through my veins, digging deep and flowing in times of hardship and uncertainty. I can say that I have been supported and looked after;

for this I am and will always be eternally grateful. Thank you. Thank you. Thank you.

I have talked about how important it is to take care of my health and well-being. I believe that by doing this I was able to deal with an abhorrent incident that happened to me earlier this year, by reacting from a place of strength and compassion. As I reflect on this, I realise that I stood in my power and reacted authentically and not how others would have expected me to have reacted. I say this because when I relayed what I had experienced, a few people said they would have acted very differently. I was not angry; I looked at the person who was disrespecting me with pity.

Racism is overt again; we have gone back in time. The narrative and chaos of the pandemic has increased fear, hatred and ignorance. Unless you are aware of the unconscious bias and the innuendos, it is very hard to understand.

"Hello. I am Sandra Moore from *** and I am here to carry out a food safety inspection. I see you have customers to serve, so I will wait until you have finished."

"Well you can't come in. Look at you. How do I know you have not got COVID? Look at you ... look at you. Have you been tested?"

As I stood there hearing her words, I saw fear in her. Never before in my life had I seen someone fearing me as if I was a monster. She had no problem serving her customers who were white. I had the authority to go ahead with the inspection, but I decided there and then that I would leave; I did not need to subject myself to her fear and ignorance. As I walked away I thought that she may have reacted that way because she had something to hide and I should have insisted on doing the inspection. My inner voice said, 'Stop making excuses for her behaviour.'

What do you see when you look at me?
A human being or just the colour of my skin?
What do you see when you look at me?
A woman who is a human being or just the colour of my skin?
What do you see when you look at me?
A woman who is a human being, who could be a mother, a daughter, a sister a
friend, a person who helps and supports others, or just the colour of my skin?
What do you see when you look at me? My light, my kindness, my love for my fellow
human beings, or just the colour of my skin?

What do you see when you look at me?
If all you see is colour then you are dehumanising
me.
When I look at you, I see your worth, your potential,
your grace, your light and, yes, I
see the colour of your skin.
When I see the colour of YOUR skin, it does not
define who you are; it is your
character, your deeds, your words, your attitude, your
behaviour, your smile, your
laughter, your kindness, the twinkle in your eye that
tells me who you are.
When I see the colour of YOUR skin, I do not fear you,
I do not instantly dislike you, I
do not use words as a weapon to try to dehumanise
you; I do NOT try to take
away your worth or dim your light to make you feel
less than.
When you look at me, see ME as a human being, see
ME as your equal; See ME
trying to survive the hate and vileness of the world
we are ALL living in.
Just as when I look at you I see you as a human
being, my equal, doing your best to
survive and thrive.

When I look at ME I see a human being who is hoping
that you recognise ME as a reflection of SELF.

Sandra Moore

Sandra started out as a Registered General Nurse before retraining and qualifying as a chartered environmental health practitioner with over thirty years' experience in food safety and health and safety.

Sandra is also passionate about health and wellness issues and is a health and well-being consultant. She launched her well-being business in autumn 2019 – Rejuvenated Soul – specialising in meditation, sound, colour and energy therapies.

Another of Sandra's loves is designing and printing T-shirts, mugs, journals and other merchandise. She is also a novice photographer, loves to travel, read, cook, walk, cycle and binge-watch good dramas. In 2018, at the age of fifty-five, she trekked one of the Inca trails which was 4,800 metres above sea level. She considers this to be one of her greatest achievements.

She has three sons and two granddaughters whom she adores.

Chapter 4.
Unlock Your Heart
Haneefah Muhammad

After eighteen months of dis-ease and stress with
sadly many lives lost
It finally looks like – at last – it might all be
changing now because
We've been told lockdown's lifting and we hope this
change is lasting –
No more distancing, elbow taps, and maybe it's
goodbye too to masking!
Not seeing family and friends for a year or more has
been really tough
Though phone calls, FaceTime and Zooms have
helped, they're not enough;
It's true that technology has kept us connected in
many different ways
But we need a human touch, not a screen, link or
password we e-generate.
So lots of people have cheered at the news of getting
back together again

Being with our families properly, with our colleagues
and out with our friends.
But there are others who feel anxious about getting
their freedom back;
They're not sure about getting back to 'normal' or
how to get back on track.
For them it's scary to think of being out and about
again and getting around;
They're struggling to imagine themselves
readjusting to life after lockdown.
If that's how you feel I'd like to share some thoughts
to help you regain
Your feelings of safety, curiosity and freedom as you
gently step out again.
First, it's OK to feel worried about going back to your
life as it was before;
You're just not sure what you may find this time
when you open the door;
But try to think of this next step as an adventure, a
journey of exploration,
A time to connect with the world using your inner
strength and your wisdom.
With so much talk of unlocking, unmasking and
getting back our freedom
Just thinking of groups may make you
uncomfortable, let alone being in them;
And it's no surprise at all to feel unsettled, uncertain
and filled with anxiety,

But focus on what's good about getting out, not what
makes you feel uneasy.
It's a simple fact that as humans we are all naturally,
instinctively social beings;
Being loved and recognised, caring and friendships
are all basic human needs;
So we need to be with other people, to share our
secrets, to laugh and to cry;
These are simple expressions of who we are and the
ways in which we thrive.
Now as you move to the 'unlocking' phase of this
ever-changing COVID journey,
Treat yourself with kindness and gently release any
feelings of doubt and worry.
Don't rush, feel at peace as you slowly embrace new
and deeper feelings of joy.
Express gratitude, trust yourself to unlock your heart
and rewrite your story.

Haneefah M

July 2021

Greetings
Wishing you
Love, Light + Peace
always. Haneefah

Haneefah Muhammad

Haneefah is a social worker and a soul empowerment coach. She believes in coaching from the 'inside-out' – connecting with our inner 'knowing' to improve relationships with the outer world.

Haneefah believes her personal experience of childhood illness and family breakdown helps her work empathically with her clients.

Haneefah runs workshops promoting mental, emotional and physical well-being for better self-care, healthier relationships and happiness. Her programme 'Speaking With Soul' is for organisations and business owners who want to be more authentic and have 'soulful-not-salesy' conversations when sharing their message with potential clients.

Haneefah is a performance poet and an author. She writes about topics such as well-being, social justice, relationships and spirituality. She co-authored *Life Inna Lockdown 2020* with the twenty-one ordinary women who contributed their extraordinary stories for the book.

Haneefah contributes to her local community through involvement in local women's groups, mental health services and arts projects.

Chapter 5.
Twelve
Natrel Mystic

Joyfully celebrating *LIL 2020* book launch
Uplifted my community with talk therapy
Learning to unburden myself
Yearning to be healed

Anger and anguish mixed with anxiety
Ugly faces on the Zoom
Gut-churning conversations
Understanding that there is a price for standing
Shut down and silenced and shouted at
Tantrums and trauma raises its head

Setting up my business
Enthusiastically avoiding confrontations
Patiently waiting for my time
Taking in my surroundings
Emotions are drained
Moving robotically through the motions
Blame myself for being available

Empty and rage for wanting it all to end again
Relax, review, rejuvenate, restart

Over it over it all
Climb higher out of the darkness
Take each step day by day
Over the hurdles it's a breakthrough
Bouncing Back to a better body
Exercising my brain
Reconstructing my life

New beginnings
Offerings to the ancestors
Volunteers value vibrate
Emit my light
Mask is off shedding my cocoon
Breaking free of the shackles
Energy renewed
Realising Eye am Natrel Mystic

Don't test me
Emotions back in check
Calmly moving towards greatness
Embody this shell of my mind
Menopause is changing my body
Beginning to feel unbalanced
Embarrassed by the hot flushes
Resonating with my elders

Jump into the new year
Aligning my chakras
New swing in my hips
Used to the feeling of my inner purpose
Appreciating each moment
Reaching out and receiving love
Yeah it's 2021

Finding my way in the world
Either way I'm moving forward
Breathe the way I've been taught
Righteously this is my space
Unanimously I vote for me
Arranging the pieces of the puzzle
Reign not rain now in the frame
Year 2 no tumour on my brain

Abundance is the gateway
Preparation is the key
Rise and shine my future awaits
I've celebrated a birthday
Lunar year set on a tray

Mighty are the Brave
Acceptance finally arrives
Younger now than I've ever felt

Justice for my people

Unity for my community
New career
Embrace all of your achievements

Just simply can't believe my luck
Underestimated my power
Lockdown didn't stop me
You're about to discover being debt-free

Again I'm here to be heard
Utmost respect for my crew
Glad we're on this journey together
Ups and downs we've got our backs
Standing firm building the trust
Talking and listening every Tuesday
Simply 2gether our new show!

Natrel Mystic

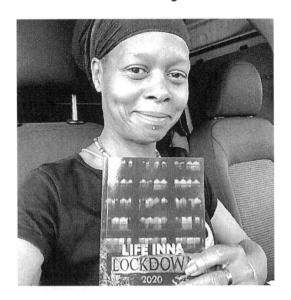

Natrel Mystic is Bouncing Back

Hiya, it's me again: Natrel Mystic. A lot has changed since the last book. It has been about knowledge, acceptance and appreciation, which are my three words. The food business changed, so look out for the new products. The new hobby became a business – I have a space in the Luton community market hub Resin8 with Rina. They say life begins at forty. I'm well into my forties and life has really just begun!

All I can say is, if you want to know how I got here, read the first book, *LIL 2020.*

Love n Lite
Learning & laughter.
Natrel Mystic ✦

Chapter 6.
Believe In You
Cecile Terrelonge

We have been in lockdown, out of lockdown and back in it more times than we ever thought would happen since April 2020. COVID-19 has affected the whole world in a way that most of us have never seen. UNPRECEDENTED. That is the word that has been used over and over again, and it is true.

COVID-19 has devastated everyone in some way. People have been ill and, sadly, died while some of us, me included, have caught it but got through it without any symptoms. It has wrecked the economy; livelihoods have been hit hard and, for some, they have not been able to come back from that. Businesses have closed never to open again, and others are hanging on by a thread. I work in the care sector and have been working throughout the pandemic, but it has been very different and strange at times. Full PPE every day has been hard but has now become my normal.

I was asked only yesterday by one of my clients, as I was leaving her home after the visit had ended, "Why don't you take off your mask as you are going?"

My reply was, "It's a habit now. I walk outside with the mask on and then put it in the bin." That's my new normal.

But change is on its way, for me and so many other people in the UK.

Due to closures and furloughs, some people have had to look for alternative employment and even changed their career paths. Some have started businesses from home, which was perhaps something they had been thinking about doing for a long time but did not want to take that step for fear of losing everything. The steps have been taken and so many are not going back to their old jobs and are continuing on their new paths.

I am about to do the same! I have been counselling children and young people for many years within the voluntary sector and it was sad to see what was happening during the pandemic.

Mental health problems in the UK population increased by sixty-nine per cent due to COVID-19, which is an alarming amount. Children and young people have suffered greatly, and I have seen an increase in the need for counselling and support to help them through this.

Their lives had completely changed: school was closed, they had to stay at home with one or two parents who may have been struggling with being furloughed or may even have lost their jobs. Domestic violence increased and, for some children who usually had school as their safe place, they found that it had been taken away from them. How do you get away from the possibility of violence daily when the country is in lockdown and you have to stay at home?

My voluntary youth counselling service moved to Zoom and continued to support young people within the community, and I had a couple of private clients via Zoom, but it was now time for me to build my private work. I have the skills and the time to support others, so I need to do this, I can do this, and I want to do this. But the imposter syndrome was setting in: you can't be a full-on counsellor; you are a voluntary counsellor working a few hours per week. You can't start a business as you already have a full-time job. What if you don't get any clients? What will you do then?

'Be brave,' is what I said to myself. 'Be brave; you've got this.' I repeated this each time I felt I was not a proper counsellor when I actually am. So, I have been brave, and I have increased my client work, I am also supporting clients from the LGBTQ community. It has been scary but exciting at the same time.

July 2020. I said that I wanted to make counselling my main job and social care my second job. Well, I have gone one step further. In a few weeks' time I will be starting a new role as a children and young persons' online counsellor with a fantastic organisation, and continuing to develop my private practice. I was brave and I took the leap to change my career.

The care sector has been my life for twenty-nine years, and I will still have the opportunity to do that, but my main focus is to help those who need it through therapy.

It may seem strange, but COVID-19 and the effect it has on the UK gave me the focus I needed to look at my own life and make the changes that are positive for me, my family and the clients I will be able to support.

One of the hardest things I have had to watch during this past year is my own daughter's mental health deteriorate and her struggle to get the support she needed. While this is now happening, I can see that others are in the same situation, and I want to be there to support them.

When lockdown came in April 2020, one of the things I said I was really going to miss was live music, because live music fills my soul with happiness and enjoyment. A few weeks ago I went to a festival; the first one in two years. There were twenty-three family and friends, and most of them I had not seen in more than two years.

We had a fantastic day. The music was great, the company was great and, for me, this is the best combination and fills my life with joy. COVID-19 was not in the front of our minds for the day and it really felt like life was starting to get back to normal.

During this unprecedented time, I've had time to reflect. I have faced my fears, and I am now going to believe in me and be the therapist I know I can be.

Cecile Terrelonge

After twenty-eight years in the care sector, I am realising my passion to be a full-time counsellor. I am going to be an online children's and young person's counsellor. I will continue to develop my private practice while supporting the Black Trans Foundation.

My two fabulous children have supported me with everything I do; we are a triangle where all three sides meet, and make an unbreakable bond.

I have been trying something new: poetry. I never thought that writing poetry would be something I would do, but it is a way of sharing my feelings, so write away, I say!

Happy reading

love

Cecile

Chapter 7.
Made for Another World
Sherell Cherish Salmon

Lockdown for me was great. My life was not particularly disrupted, which I enjoyed. I'm not a fan of humans and going outside, so being stuck indoors was a breeze. I was recovering from the death of my mentor, so I started lockdown having bereavement counselling, which was helpful. I had quite a productive lockdown and was more sociable. I did home-made quizzes – my friends and I were truly tested on how well we knew each other. We had online parties and festivals and I think it's safe to say being in lockdown gave me the worst hangovers of my life. The virus didn't bother me as I'm a germaphobe, so was using hand sanitiser way before it was cool.

There are two passions in my life: writing and astronomy. When I was four I wanted to be a writer and then, at the age of eight, my passion for space and planets developed. I thought I had to make a choice;

however, I have learnt to combine the two. I designed a web page for the spacecraft Herschel during my year ten work experience at the Royal Greenwich Observatory. I also wrote blogs and articles on astrophysics for the Royal Astronomical Society. This led me to write about my experiences of having mental health and trying to follow my dreams.

The most appealing feature about astrophysics is the way that complex physical phenomena can be explained by simple and elegant theories. I enjoy the logical aspect of the subject and I find it very satisfying when all the separate pieces of a problem fall together to create one simple theory. My interest and aptitude for mathematics adds an extra dimension to studying astrophysics and I relish the challenge of a complicated problem both in physics and mathematics.

Lockdown helped me to realise what direction I want to move towards, in my life. This has been a year for me to gain skills and push myself out of my comfort zone. I used the year to teach myself more coding. Although I learnt the basics during my studies, I wanted to become more advanced. During this time, I was asked to do a podcast after someone read my article 'Astronomy, BPD & Me' from the RAS, Astronomy and Geophysics Forum.

After this podcast was released, a lady contacted me who runs a networking company called Simply Deez Events, which includes a group of people who motivate, inspire and support within a community which started in Luton. Being part of this group has helped me to gain confidence by participating in some of their projects, which includes being assigned to be the production manager/lead on the Simply Well project we run in conjunction with the Recovery College Luton and Bedfordshire.

The podcast also enabled me to feature on all of Bromley, Lewisham and Greenwich social media and their website.

2020 seemed to be a great year for me mentally. Like, come on – I only overdosed once, which is a big deal for me. Things were going pretty well until everything came crashing down around me on February the 9th 2021. My mummy died after slipping on ice on the way to work.

Mummy dying was/is the worst experience of my life. I always said that I wanted to die first, so I have spent majority of my life taking overdoses and being admitted into psychiatric hospitals. I understand that no parent should ever lose a child, but I do not believe in this. She had people; I only had her. Now she has gone, I have no one. People say they are there, but they can only be there to a certain point, which then reminds me I do not have anyone really.

I have an amazing therapist who was around before Mummy died. She helps me to understand why I get so frustrated with humans. I have certain expectations which I follow and expect others to follow, so when someone diverts and goes off course, it messes with my mind and I can't handle it. Basically, I see things in black and white and there is no grey/middle area. I like plans and to follow rules; however, humans are unpredictable, and I feel society expects me to adjust, whereas I want people to adjust to my simple ways, which isn't going to happen, and this is where I don't fit in the world. My thought process is so rigid, and I know a lot of people don't get it, but at least my therapist understands.

It's like when someone asks me for a favour and tells me I can say no. But when I say no, they don't like my answer as they really wanted me to say yes, and they are someone who encourages me to do what I feel and don't say yes to please others, but when I follow their advice, they turn on me. So, it makes me feel I should just please others. It's like going one step forward, two steps back as my confidence gets knocked.

Also, don't tell me you'll call me back if you're not going to call back. Don't say the time is 08:30 when it's

08:27. This is how my autistic mind works and it stresses me out when things aren't accurate. To me, this means you have lied and with a lie comes lack of trust, which is why I have trust issues. I find it difficult to know what people are thinking, but I care way too much about what people are feeling.

Every day I wake up hoping to die as I don't feel that I have a reason to live. However, ultimately in the future, I want a husband; someone to love me as much as I love them. A job that makes me look forward to getting up every morning. I hope it will involve writing, tutoring and just sharing my life experiences, encouraging young minds and inspiring them to believe in themselves and follow their dreams.

Sherell Cherish Salmon

Sherell is a young lady lost throughout her life and trying to find her place in the world. Born in Bromley, Kent, Sherell has always loved to write and, since the age of eight, has been fascinated by astrophysics, which inspired her to continue her passion into adulthood. She was diagnosed with selective mutism at the age of three which later in life brought on a diagnosis of autism level two. She also has mental illness, which she has suffered from since a young age. Her diagnoses are emotionally unstable personality disorder, aka borderline personality disorder, clinical depression, social anxiety, OCD and self-harm.

Sherell has a bachelor's degree in astronomy, space science and astrophysics obtained at the University of Kent, Canterbury, and a master's degree in astrophysics obtained at University College London.

Dedicated to my mummy, Pauline Salmon (10/4/1961–9/2/2021). Love you always and forever xXx **https://linktr.ee/SCSalmon**

Chapter 8.
It Is What It Is
Kieron Mongan

Here are a couple of statistics I learnt the other day:

150,000 people DIE every day around the world.

385,000 babies are BORN every day around the world.

I prefer the positive stats!

March 2020. The start of lockdown, and I found myself jobless, living with my mum and single. I did have some cash, though, so I thought to myself, 'I'm not gonna panic and get another DEAD-END job. I'll seek out new opportunities instead.'

My interests for financial growth were trading, investing and property. Through COVID I took some education, picked up some skills for life, made investments and connected with like-minded people. I still to this day talk to them about goals and aspirations. The abundance seed was planted and I trust God has me right where I'm meant to be in my journey to success.

Success is the progressive realisation of a worthy goal or ideal (Earl Nightingale).

As of today, COVID has taken 4.55 million lives. How staggering is that?

I'm lucky to have a loving mum, Jackie, who would do anything for her kids. She's done more for me than I could ever have asked for. I have two siblings, Rachael and Daniel, whom I admire and love. They only want the best for me; they have seen me laugh in life and they have seen me break down in life. I know deep down all they want is for me to be happy. I'm trying – one per cent better each day is one of my many mottos!

Anyway, if you're reading this, you have survived the pandemic, so you don't need me to tell you what you already know. It's been horrific for all of us. It's brought us all closer and reminded us what is important in life – toilet roll!

Jokes aside, when I walk the streets now, the world feels like a better place. We all seem to show more love to our fellow man, which is what God wants: Love thy Neighbour as thyself (Matthew 22:39).

During COVID, I attended a course called peer mentorship. I'm hopeful to get involved with positive and impactful projects that can help those in need. I also have my own YouTube channel where I've done videos on good and bad days. I'm not diagnosed with anything; I don't think there's a label they can find for me! I'll just make my own and call it Kieron!

I've also been very fortunate to connect with some great people during COVID: Dee Choto; Tatti Marongwe; Pam Thompson; Dee Bailey; Rita James; Matthew Winchester and many more. Whether direct or in a group, I've drawn on the wisdom of others, humbled myself as a student, always been open to advice and ready to say YES to opportunity. I am an opportunist! That's helped get me in this book.

Funny story. Me and Mum had some great teamwork going during COVID; she would go to Iceland and Aldi to do the food shop with a few bags, and I would ride up on my bike when she was finished. It was a smooth arrangement, most of the time. There was this one day though, when I met my mum at Aldi, picked up the two bags and off I went. Riding along and I get just before my turn on Ashton New Road, which is a main road, and bumf, snap, wallop! Both bags snap and on the road was ham, cheese, milk, teacakes, coleslaw, you name it, everywhere on the road! I didn't panic; I actually laughed! So I get the stuff in the bags while a queue of cars are waiting for me, but problem was the two big bags had snapped. I'm struggling, walking with my bike and my bags along the path. All of a sudden, this car pulls over and a random woman jumps out of her car, takes out a couple of plastic bags and runs over and says, "There you go mate!"

I learnt two things that day: in a crisis I can laugh and, also, there is goodness in this world!

I'll leave with a poem. I love creative things such as poetry, the spoken word, art, graffiti and much more. We all have the capability to create something authentic, that's my belief.

I remember the day when COVID broke
some people took it as a joke
what's this in China goin' on?
Some bat in a market, what's gone wrong?
As days went by the numbers rise
the spread went further and wide
eventually it become worldwide
the toilet roll at first was prioritised
but with the jokes set aside
the face masks on we sanitised
the daily news we felt paralysed
negative news was at its highest high
fuck off COVID I personally would say
with all the chaos takin' place

new-born heroes were workin' away
frontline NHS saving lives
essential services still provide
we all got together and clapped outside
when the clock struck eight on Thursday nights
a sense of togetherness and pride
all different walks of life collide
in each other we could confide
In this together, vast and wide
this horrible virus could kill us all
stand together one and all
the vaccine was made and here we are
be grateful you have come this far
4.55 million lives taken so far
this pandemic really set the bar
get your jabs, both of them and say ta-ra
go on that holiday and get straight to the bar!

I'm honoured and humbled to be in this book and to be part of the *Life Inna Lockdown* family!

Peace be with you.

Kieron Mongan

Kieron is thirty-five, from Manchester, and has been a salesman for the last decade. He is very keen to get involved in impactful projects to help others in need, such as community projects and voluntary work. He is at the start of a new and exciting journey to be the best version of himself and is a self-confirmed opportunist!

Chapter 9.
I Am Not Superwoman
Dee Bailey

The good old Zoom proved to be a lifeline like no other. I was asked in August 2020, "How is it going? This whole lockdown thing?" The person had their head down and I said, feeling quite embarrassed to be honest, "Really good." The first book, *Life Inna Lockdown 2020: Behind Closed Doors*, was published in July.

My world was changing around me and personally. Was it such a bad thing? Working from home was enjoyable. I loved it. The positives: saving on petrol, not having to get up and travel to work, on occasions being able to look after my grandchildren more, no bra (if you know, you know).

Negatives – weight gain, being unfit, missed seeing family and friends and the physical events! Just getting out the house.

As leader of Simply Deez Events I have to keep it real and say that I look at everyone as part of my flock. Sometimes I feel so guilty that I have not contacted who I wanted to, not had that conversation, message exchange. Then I remind myself, I am not superwoman. There are only twenty-four hours in a day.

Opportunities are always there, it's whether we decide to grab them. COVID has at times made me feel fearless. With a 'just do it, make it happen' attitude. People are asking me why, where I found the strength to keep going during this period and, if I am honest, it's the love and encouragement from the Simply Deez Events/LIL Crew, people I don't even know. When someone says, "Thank you for the work you do for the community of Luton." I have not seen this person for over fifteen years! How do you know what I've been up to? Good old social media.

Oct 2020. The Community Pop Up Space, now called the Community Hub & Collaborative Store, was born. Who would have known a simple idea would lead to so many new connections! Closed, open, closed, open. Ha-ha. "I bet you wished you had not opened it during COVID?" I was asked. Not at all. I'm so glad we did. A space for organisations to utilise with information and for small business to promote and sell their products.

1 Jun. Simply 2Gether Show is launched. The vision of an online magazine show was born. Whoop 5 lady anchors. Every Tuesday, 12-12.30 p.m. A mix of chat, conversation, with different guests each week.

Late June – I receive a Certificate of Appreciation from the former Mayor of Luton, Councillor Maria Lovell. I was reminded that not everyone enjoys your wins, not everyone is in your corner. I am not fooled into thinking, 'Everyone loves Dee Bailey,' what you do and what you stand for. You cannot be everyone's cup of tea, otherwise you would not do anything.

So just a few things under the Simply Deez Events Umbrella:

Life Inna Lockdown Zoom

RealTalk with Simply Deez – Talk show

Simply Well – In Partnership with Bedfordshire recovery College

Simply 2gether Show

Community Hub & Collaborative Store

International Women's Day Celebration

International Men's Day Celebration

The Black Bookcase

Simply Deez Warriors – Relay for Life

LIL – get-together

Theatre Trip

The last few months have been hard. I'm not entirely sure why, but it's like when you get the feeling you are on a roundabout and someone keeps spinning and spinning and spinning and you want to get off. Just for a while, not permanently. When you give a lot, people expect a lot more than you can give sometimes. I know that I am not superwoman, but yet I still have to keep telling myself that. Some mornings I wake up, give thanks and then 'shake off' the invisible cape. How many times do we hear people say, and I have said it many a time myself, "You can't pour from an empty cup." I know I need to take more time to recharge and just breathe. Some may call it being selfish, but self-care is a must.

The foundation of a legacy is being built for others to continue.

What's next? Africa is waiting for me, to visit, to live, who knows? Gotta reach there first and see. Life is the adventure we make it, and we have to work with the cards we are dealt.

While I can, I am going to grab the opportunities with both hands. I do not want the regrets: what if? Should I? I am totally embracing my truly amazing innings. Gratitude is a must, thanking the most high, family, friends and the Simply Deez/LIL Crew who have supported and believe in the vision. A building is coming!

Dee Bailey

Dee Bailey is Founder/CEO of Simply Deez Events. The organisation is 6.5 years old. Very much a visionary, if there is such a word, and has been working in the community for over twenty-three years. Passionate about the community and making a difference. I believe if we can ChangelLife we can possibly SavelLife.

Chapter 10.
You Kept Me Here For a Reason
Rita James

Every day I sit and think about the people and family I have lost and just didn't know if I could carry on.

The hurt I felt was like I broke my leg again; the pain was so bad, but that pain/leg got fixed. My family do not know I cry every other day, because of the grief I feel from losing the best parents we could have had and then losing two sisters as well. I thought, 'God, why do you take the best? I wanted you to take me,' because this hurt I felt was unreal. I go to your graves often; I sit and talk to you all and tell you I meet the most amazing and inspirational people on Zoom.

They are the reason I am still here, because I can really talk to them, tell them how I am truly feeling, cry and swear never to be judged by anyone.

There were so many times I said to myself, while crying in my chair, 'I just cannot do this any more.'

Then I would get a text, "Rita, can you help us raise money for this person/cause?" This is the reason again you kept me here. It broke my heart meeting them, but helping was my reward. I got to see this person, now smiley and making memories the best they could.

But the main reason you kept me here was that my family needed me; they are not ready to see me go yet. I don't believe God is ready to meet me yet: for the words that come out of my mouth, I would burn.

It's true when they say you only get one life, because my life changed big time when I had to fight a rare sarcoma cancer. It was horrific, but the reason I'm still here is the laughter I gave the other patients in hospital. A smile was the greatest gift of all, as I knew some of them I would never see again.

Yes I am in pain 24/7, but you wouldn't know that if you saw me. Some say, "You look good Rita," but underneath I feel like crying. But my family are great warriors and never give up.

I was raised by the most inspirational parents and have the best brothers and sisters I could ever ask for, but we do say we should have our own hospital, because we keep the NHS going. There are so many health issues in the family, but we never give up.

There is always support when any one of us needs it and I'm very lucky to have what I have.

I have always raised my kids to never judge by just looking at someone, because there is always a story behind someone's smile or the way they look and dress. And this is the reason you kept me here, so I can carry on helping others, because there is nothing better than when someone says, "Thank you. Kind words can help so many."

Believe me, I'm not scared to stand up and stand my ground for myself or others. My brothers said I should have been the fourth brother.

I was told by my professors in London I'm a walking miracle because not many survive rare sarcoma cancers like mine, along with the high-intensity treatment I went through and everything I am going through now.

I look back and wonder how I coped with all of it. I have fibrosis now that I didn't know I had from the treatment because I never read the small print on the letters; just another load of appointments. It will never get better. It could stay as it is if I'm lucky or it could get worse and I'll end up needing a transplant.

I wrote letters to everyone – they are in my filing box – because I really didn't know if I would still be here.

Even my speech to read out in church, as up in heaven my name is Karma and I am coming to get you. I AM going to ring that bell and say I beat cancer, and ring it for all those that tried to fight this horrific disease.

I have to say that it was the nurses, doctors and professors that kept me here. The care I received and continue to receive is outstanding, including even the cleaner. I thanked all of the people who would go out of their way to bring my breakfast because, going through cancer, you go off many things (I couldn't even drink tea). Nothing was too much trouble for them.

That's another reason I am still here: the NHS really has saved me. I am still fighting, but every day I say, "No goodbyes today!"

When my sister Margaret was taken into hospital on a Sunday night, I had to work Monday on a late shift (at Tesco). My senior team member said, "Rita, go and be with your sister in hospital." I said there wouldn't be anyone on the department but he said, "Just go." I owe this man the most respect, because if Steve Rixon did not send me out to be with my sister, I would never have been able to tell Margaret just how much she meant to me and thank her for what she had done for the whole family. Because of Steve, I was able to spend all day and night with her. I will never forget him, because not all managers are compassionate like him.

Every day I wake up and thank God for another day. Every day is a special day. I need to tell my family how I really feel, instead of talking to other people, because I really do have the best.

My friend Pip means so much to me, as she is the only one that can try to tell me off. She used to say to me, "Don't you dare give up!"

She said a few other things but, haha, I can't write them here, so I will have to think about writing my book.

Rita James

My name is Rita James. I was born in London. Mum and Dad were both Catholic Irish, and there were eight of us. I have been with my hubby for thirty-four years and have four children: three boys and one girl.

I regularly volunteer for a few charities – Mary Seacole, Cancer Research UK, Hospice at Home, Meaningful Education, Bedfordshire Community Police Projects, and support many more whenever help is needed.

So this is my story. My first chapter in book one was called My Never-Ending Story. I hope you enjoy this new chapter.

Chapter 11.
What Next? Bring It On
Shelley (Michelle) Titmus

I said when *Life Inna Lockdown* book one came out that book two would be coming, and here it is. I have had to re-read my last piece to remember just where I left off, because I don't know about you, but the weeks and months of COVID have gone by really fast AND really slow. It's been some kind of weird suspended time, which then goes fast-forward to catch up.

So, in May 2020, things had started to settle and we all found new ways to carry on, with people starting to open services, shops, schools and businesses. That meant, for me, my husband Will was still working from our home and, in fact, while writing this in August 2021 he has only just gone back to his office (I had better mention the hubby this time, because I forgot in last book, haha). I, thankfully, could still run my bakery business from home with socially distanced deliveries that put smiles on faces. I think

I'm going to refer back to my piece in book one, with each part updated.

My mum in Weymouth – It took me until June 2021 to make it down to see my mum. We waited until I was double-vaccinated and we both felt safe. We definitely couldn't see each other before we were allowed to hug (we are huggers). Mum has kept well on her own, with supermarket deliveries and all the residents around where she lives helping each other out. Mum has attended Zoom feeds for church and, unfortunately, a funeral, but she is getting on so well with her laptop and keeping up with what's going on, I'm so proud.

Families United Network – I mentioned I was a trustee at this charity that provides activities and respite care for children and adults with additional needs. All the way through, we have followed the same bubble system as schools and other healthcare providers. I am glad to say we have now opened our doors as usual to our families for their school holiday club. I work in the coffee shop, and I loved this summer hearing and seeing the building full of laughter, play and chatter from both children and the adults. We are still keeping everyone safe with COVID testing, but all the usual activities and madness are back, and it feels great.

My mental health and suicide awareness training – I am still learning, still advocating and raising awareness of all mental health issues and how you can help. I am constantly sharing on social media of how we can help each other. I last attended lots of Zooms with charities (mainly the OLLIE Foundation – One Life Lost Is Enough – suicide awareness/intervention training), but I went one step further and I am now an official mental health first aider trained by The Mental Health Foundation. My take on learning all of this information is that it is just like medical first aid: you learn it just in case, to help someone in the future.

This, to me, is exactly the same, as I work in the community a lot. I might be able to help and signpost them to the services they need. This is something I believe will be needed more as we come out of COVID. Many of those that were already affected by their mental health before the lockdown have actually enjoyed the change of staying at home, which became their safe place with no constant interaction. Or people that need to be around others with social and physical interaction have suddenly had it taken away from them for way longer than we thought. Both these and all the others that have NOW felt this since the lockdowns are going to have a hard transition in this coming year and beyond. Sorry to be clichéd, but: "It's

OK not to be OK", "If you can be anything, be kind", "It's good to talk", "Ask if they are OK and ask if they are REALLY OK", "Listen to hear and learn, not listen to respond".

Last but not least, Simply Deez Events – Now CIC. Yes, it's OFFICIAL: we are now a COMMUNITY INTEREST COMPANY. Dee started her events business in 2014 and I have been involved since 2016. I was only helping out when I could and joining all of the different events. We have all said Dee needed to go official and now, during lockdown, after all the Zoom calls and gathering the community/family together as much as possible, she has finally done it. She has also gone and made me the additional director!

So, when people ask what you want to do with your life ... take that chance, grab with both hands and run with it, even though it may feel like madness.

As part of the crazy journey since lockdown, we have a community of Zoom calls and are still doing virtual events to replace our usual live ones (like international men's and women's days and our Black Bookcase events). The biggest thing we have done so far is open up a market stall in Luton Indoor Market. This is both a community hub for people to gather and gain information (whether by people from various charities/organisations or picking up leaflets), and also small independent businesses renting shelf space with us to sell their products (we man the stall, take payments and update social media adverts). Knowing Dee, this is just the beginning, with a proper building to cover all this in the future.

So, the future. Nothing is going to be the same again. Remember how, after 9/11, airports and their checks changed, and now it's normal? I can see similar for the years to come with COVID, but no one knows what that will look like. So I will just hang on tightly to the here and now, and the roller coaster of whatever comes next. Nothing is a given and anything can happen to keep you on your toes.

Shelley (Michelle) Titmus

Married underwater in Florida in 1999
to Will with a fur baby called TJ.

I have my own bakery business run from home since 2014 called ShelleyScrumptious, and I'm now director of Simply Deez Events CIC.

All my life I have been involved in the community in various roles, latterly within certain areas due to my own personal circumstances. I am an advocate for infertility, cancer awareness and fundraising (Relay for Life Luton / CRUK and Pancreatic Cancer UK), autism and 'dis'abilities, suicide awareness, mental health/wellness/well-being and hidden illnesses, all of which can be connected in many ways.

Chapter 12.
And We Never Knew
Munyaradzi Sajanga

We never knew that going to work and going back home without being told what to do was a favour of the Almighty.

We often complained about going to work; we never knew we were privileged to still be employed and wake up every morning to go to work. We never knew that spending time with our families, friends, and colleagues, sharing experiences about life together would one day be restricted and we would be forced to isolate from any human contact. Leaving our homes for official engagements, businesses, trade, vocation, family gatherings, going to church and any sort of events were all restricted. The only way you were allowed out was if it was necessary. One wondered what 'necessary' was and it was not easy to decide, so this had to be spelled out to everyone.

Whoever thought that taking a walk down the street freely and meeting up with friends or loved ones in the other towns would one day be prohibited. Getting public transport, sharing a seat with strangers was a thing of the past, and you needed to mask up everywhere you went. Meeting people, standing close to them, hugging, shaking hands and all that we once called normal became prohibited.

At first it was difficult to follow all these rules, but then fear caused everyone to adhere to the guidelines set out by the government.

COVID-19 denies us our liberty. It kept us away from our families, friends, colleagues, and the rest of the world. What used to be normal was now abnormal.

One day this disease knocked on my own door. I have never been so scared in my life. All I could do was pray to God for healing across my household. I watched my partner suffering from this disease. I didn't know how to help him, and to make sure he was comfortable and well fed. Even as a big food lover, it became apparent that eating or drinking was uncomfortable.

I became very wary of his condition. News channels were flooded with statistics of the number of people who were dying and the rate at which new infections were rising. In my mind, it still felt like a dream until I saw it in my own home and my partner's suffering.

All I could do was get on my knees and pray to my God and my ancestors to heal him and get rid of his pain.

Not long after, news of my fellow countrymen started to come in. It was one story after another. A Zimbabwean nurse died – someone I knew as a friend and customer. A few days later, another Zimbabwean died, from right here in our own town of Luton. He was an accountant I knew.

It was only then it started to sink in that this COVID monster is real and it's out there devouring the young, old, rich and poor. These life-changing events changed my perspective towards life in general and how I carried myself. It gave me a wake-up call that tomorrow is not guaranteed. It could easily be me or my partner or someone in my family who vacates this world next.

I got scared and my mental health was affected deeply. Life has taken me through some really rough patches, but in those rough situations there would always be a glimmer of hope.

Then came COVID; it was a situation in which I could not see that glimmer of hope. Scientists, doctors, politicians, even religious leaders seemed to not have a clue how or when this monster would end.

There is something about being hopeless in a situation while you watch your loved ones suffer. It's like you have been incapacitated and there is nothing you can do to help make the situation better.

Days passed, then at one point it became really bad for my partner and I was left with no choice but to call for an ambulance. They came to attend to him. They did some tests and there was good and bad news. The good news was he did not have the South African COVID variant, which was the worst at the time. The bad news was that he still had the virus, nonetheless.

I kept thinking that I told him not to go to South Africa, but he insisted on going. He must have thought COVID was just like every other kind of flu and he was Superman, so he could not catch anything. I was furious at him, but at the same time scared.

However, I kept my hope and faith that he would endure the pain and it would pass. Then I started thinking: what about me and our son in our household? What about his friends and everyone he has been in contact with?

The questions in my head were endless, and I had a lot of sleepless nights where I prayed the sun would come out and everything would be back to normal.

Eventually he got better and back on his feet. I thank God that we are still here to tell the story.

Business was the last thing to worry about during those times; the most important thing became staying alive. Staying alive was now a huge achievement for me, but my business suffered a lot. I had to work from home. Thankfully, I managed to keep it going, but it was hard. Being a small business makes it even more challenging due to the lack of resources that most big companies have.

I must say my business is very fortunate to have survived, and I am grateful. Most businesses have shut down because they could not sustain themselves during the lockdown.

The horrible thing about this pandemic is not being able to plan in advance, as no one knows when it will end.

We never knew. And still we are uncertain if we will ever go back to normal or adjust to the new normal.

Munyaradzi Sajanga

Munya is a businesswoman who runs a group of companies offering many services, from transport, entertainment, goodwill ambassadors to health and well-being. She enjoys being around other people who are like-minded. She is a member of various women's groups that help other women in the community.

Munya is a Zimbabwean, a mother, who came to live in the UK some twenty years ago. She has adopted and learnt a lot from living in this country and will one day take all this knowledge and pass it on to inspiring young entrepreneurs. She is always encouraging young people to be creative and aspire to be their own bosses.

Chapter 13.
And It Began
Remie Dominique

I don't think anybody knew just how much life was going to change. Lockdown started and everything else stopped. No more quick trips to friends' houses. No more, "Just running to the shops; would you like anything?" Everything stopped.

Although I work at the hospital and worked every day through the pandemic, I've heard it a million times: "It can't be that much of a change for you." It was, in a way that I never expected. I became comfortable; more comfortable than I thought I would. I had my family around me and we bonded in a way I never thought we would.

I became so much closer to my brother. He became my best friend. We did everything together. Granted, that was only activities that could be performed within the four walls of our house, but we did everything together. And I loved it.

Until the pandemic ended, I hadn't realised that my perception of time was completely thrown off, and my perception of real life had been thrown off. In my head, this was forever and nothing would change. I knew from the beginning that my brother would move out again, like he had many times before, but in our little lockdown bubble that hadn't even crossed my mind.

I got to know him. I got to know his autism. We'd never been closer. I felt protective of him and, in a selfish way, didn't feel that anybody else would understand him the same way. But he moved, and although that day was hard and I knew we wouldn't be just our little bubble any more, I watched him flourish.

We stayed as close as we had been, just in different houses. I visited him and got to know his friends on a completely new level and felt more accepted by new people than I ever had. I felt like I was still protecting him and he was protecting me, just in new bubbles.

After he moved, I started to realise my anxiety was not just about losing our bubble: it was about everything. I wanted to see my friends so badly. I wanted to be out in the world enjoying life how I used to, but something was holding me back. Everything seemed so scary. I could not make sense of the ever-changing rules, on what was and wasn't allowed. It didn't make sense to me.

I started off slowly, going to friends' houses again, only in small groups, just to test the waters, and I felt fine. Then I branched out to the pubs and restaurants. 'Eat out to help out' and all that, and I felt fine. Then, on to parties and holidays, and I felt absolutely fine. In fact, I felt amazing. I had longed for this all back from the beginning. I had felt like I had lost my independence when this all started; my opportunities to get away and live my life to the fullest, create memories with friends and just feel free.

But there was something in the back of my mind that I just could not shift. Then came the onslaught of lockdown after lockdown, restriction after restriction. It just didn't stop. My age group were the problem. 'Eat out to help out' was the problem. Everything but the virus was the problem. You couldn't do right for doing wrong. It carried on for so long.

Like many other people, I had my birthday in lockdown, which was strange. I didn't mind, because that anxiety was still in my head. Well, not just my head – I had started to break. I thought it might have been just the constant lockdowns affecting my mental health, not being able to see people face to face affecting my depression. I was withdrawn, I was tired.

But there was no definite answer, so that was that. I carried on. I felt blow after blow, with my driving tests being cancelled, working non-stop, being stuck inside. I just wanted it to end.

I took test after test at work and at home. I even had my vaccine in the hope we would be free again. And it came. Lockdown was over and we were FREE! But I wasn't. I still felt all these emotions; they were affecting me daily. I couldn't talk to people. I didn't want to see or be seen by people. I was crying at work every day. I was exhausted. My mental health took everything from me and all I wanted was to curl up in a ball and stop existing.

This couldn't just be because of the pandemic? Surely not? It was all over the news: mental health had been affected nationwide, but not in the way I was feeling. It was intense. It felt like, every day, someone was squeezing me hoping I would burst. And I burst ...

I was diagnosed with PTSD. I never thought I would hear the words, PTSD. What does that mean? How can that be me? What do I do now? I'm young and have my whole life ahead of me yet I'm stuck not knowing what to do. I'm scared to sleep because of the nightmares; I'm scared to be at work in case someone finds me.

And then it hit me: I've been scared. This whole time I've been scared; scared of what's to come, scared of the new, scared of the old. I don't want to be scared any more. I am strong, I am brave and I am free. Free of the past, free to be the best person I can be.

I'm struggling every day, but I'm trying. Every day is hard but I know that the good days are coming. I no longer have to fear the 'what ifs' because I am living now. That's something I didn't think I would be able to say.

I'm living each day as it comes and, no matter how hard it may feel, I have my support behind me and future ahead of me.

Remie Dominique

Hello. I'm Remie Dominique. I'm a 23-year-old photographer and videographer who is still trying to spread some happiness and strength in the world.

I am a strong believer in taking everything as it comes and turning it into a lesson I can learn from. While I was at university, I became a survivor of domestic abuse. From that I have been diagnosed with PTSD. I'm just taking every day as it comes and finding the light in every situation.

I hope that I will be able to finish the documentary I started so that I can still help people understand and advocate for young people suffering with mental health and domestic abuse situations. As always, I want to help people find their safe space within themselves so that they can become the best person they can be and not be afraid of the stigma of mental health, but embrace themselves as a whole person.

Chapter 14.
I Don't Want to Write About Lockdown
Leah Bailey

Everyone is reflecting
on the last
6 months
of not seeing
friends and family.
But thanks to
webcam programs
I've seen
more friends
more family
more often
than any other
6 months … ever.
Because people are
more willing
more available
more still
more aware

of how important
seeing is.

Over 24 weeks
of wondering
what next week
will bring ...
of seeing the wishes
of people
who wanted
a never-ending
weekend
granted.
All blends together
until schedules
are lost
and the 172 days
begin to lose
their meaning
and I try to find
a reason to get up.

Everyone is reflecting
and writing
and reading
and knitting
and learning
new languages

new skills
new hobbies
new music
new films
new shows ...
4,128 hours
of trying to fill
gaps previously filled
with the rat race
deadliness
appointments, alarms
and snooze buttons
too much time now
to know what we did.

I don't want to reflect
on how much
this isn't affecting me
as it should.
I don't want to write
about spending
247,680 minutes
not climbing the walls,
not missing
my commute,
not feeling put out
by not going out,
not feeling any more lonely

than usual,
not feeling guilt
about not learning
new skills
not finishing that unfinished novel
no guilt about
no guilt or interest.
If I don't think about
Lockdown,
If I don't write about
Lockdown,
I won't worry
about my heart
crying out alone
in these months
weeks, days, minutes
any more than
the decades of fellowship
and love
of family and friends
before now
(and hopefully after)
these 14,860,800 seconds
that have consumed
the consciousness
of the world
to the exclusion of millennia.

26/08/2020

Despite what I say in verse four, there is no resisting it; no stopping the reflection on the paradigm shift in the world. I don't want to, but I have to. We all do. Deciding what parts of the 'new' world we want to keep, what parts need to go; what parts of the 'old' world we want to resurrect, what parts we need to excise (or exorcise as may be). I was lucky enough to be in a 'key worker' job, teaching, which meant my life was not as impacted as others. My day to day was more normal than most. Whether it was online or face to face – well, PPE-covered face to PPE-covered face – I was teaching ... doing too much work at too short notice with no time or help outside of the staff and admin at my school, who were my colleagues in the trenches. Everyone wanting answers and no one having them about lessons, technology, socialisation and exams. Somehow, like always, we got it done. Twice. I can only hope the new-found, long-overdue appreciation of parents for what exactly teachers do will last. Though I'm reasonably sure it won't.

I'm not what anyone would class as an introvert; I thrive in social situations. Not only do I thrive, but I gain immense self-worth and self-esteem from gathering people together, creating communities in my home, feeding people and fostering friendship and conversation over huge meals. So, the loss of the ability to have people in my house for big meals and gatherings was great. Simultaneously, it was a relief. I do love hosting and making sure people I love are having a good time, but not being allowed to let me off the hook, out of the responsibility I enjoy so much. An enforced vacation that I still can't decide if I liked, or benefited from. Just like my job, my socialisation moved online exclusively in the beginning and mostly stayed that way even after things began to open up. I didn't miss the restaurants or the pubs, not in and of themselves, not the way everyone else seemed to. I've never felt so odd, so weird, so freakish as when I realised I wasn't suffering the loss of that kind of freedom everyone else seemed to be. Online contact, convenient and almost constant, was enough for me.

In fact, online contact expanded my life in ways I never could have predicted. First and foremost, it connected me more frequently with my family, 3,500 miles away. I can only afford to go home once a year, and I usually choose Christmas and New Year to enjoy the family traditions around that time.

As bad luck would have it, I didn't go home during the holidays in 2019 because I was supposed to go for a family reunion in July of 2020 and my usual Christmas trip in 2020. Obviously, neither of those things happened, which was more tragic than I can say. Two close family members passed at about the time I was supposed to be there; I could do nothing but wish I had made it over to help and comfort.

Despite this, being able to talk and share news regularly is one of those habits I intend to keep. I feel closer and more connected to their lives than I have for years. I wish tragedy and emergency hadn't been necessary to realise how much I needed this.

Though tragedy had struck, there has also been triumph, and this online revolution had its role in that too. In May of 2020 I published my first collection of poetry; something I'd wanted to do for more than twenty-five years. My dream had not included having to promote it exclusively online, but necessity is the mother of invention. I dove into the waters of social media and online events and discovered a web there to catch me; a network of soulmates and fellow creatives I'd never have found otherwise. From one event to another, one link in the chain to the next. A changed world, a chain of connections, spreading further than anything else.

I choose to focus on that. I choose to keep that as my enduring memory of the lockdown – that which was found, NOT what was lost.

Leah Bailey

R aised in the US but living permanently in the UK since 2003, Leah has an international point of view. As a teacher of English language and literature for more than ten years, and as a writer of poetry and fiction for more than twenty-five, Leah has dedicated her life to the written word and its ability to inspire and connect people.

Leah holds degrees in English, comparative literature and international studies from Pennsylvania State University in the United States, as well as a minor in

German language and literature. At Canterbury Christ Church University, Leah trained for a Postgraduate Certificate in Education in teaching secondary English, media studies and drama.

Most days are spent sharing her passion for the written word with young people, trying to comprehend British slang and making sure her coffee cup is never empty, for the health and safety of others.

Chapter 15.
The Graduation
Take Nothing for Granted,
It All Counts!
Nike Akiti

You did not pass, you did not fail, you did not leave the class! A popular saying from my Nigerian youth, meaning you did not progress, randomly popped into my head when someone asked me if I was still in customer services. It was an innocent question from someone I had not seen for a long time, but the question got me thinking. On the surface it appears true; it looks like there has been no progression in my life since July 2020. I still hate my job and I am still in it. I have still not made the home improvements I have desired for a long time. I should feel like an abject failure.

However, being in lockdown has served to reinforce my belief in 'everything in God's time'. During this and the first lockdown, reflection became my new best friend. I share these three things that are of importance to me:

1, Gratitude: There are many things for which I am extremely grateful, but I speak about my job, about which I can say with confidence I love and hate in equal measure because it takes up a big chunk of my waking day. It kept me at home like I was not home, which I found to be very frustrating. But I love talking to people, helping them with their issues, which is what the job entails, but I hate the micromanagement enabled by the big brother of modern technology; the same technology that allowed me to be home.

I am genuinely grateful that having this job means the basic stuff remains the basic stuff, and I do not have to worry. It means my focus can be on what is important to me. This technology – FaceTime, WhatsApp and Zoom – I am still grateful they are on my list of top tools, as they kept me in touch (I thank God for you. You know who you are – much love).

I often feel guilty for disliking the job so, but I also feel with the prevalence of social media and our 24-hour connectivity culture, there is a lot of pressure to feel grateful, when in actuality one might feel anxious, fearful or just downright fed up of the situation. For some of the time, that should be OK too.

2. People and sensibility: I admit, where before I wouldn't have, I am now more sensitive than I ever gave myself credit for. I noted that even in a pandemic we would still quarrel with our mates, family will not be bothered about you the way you might think, and work would make unnecessary and often difficult or unjust demands on you. This would knock me out of sorts.

I was privileged to meet lots of new people and hear many stories, from which I drew inspiration and a feeling of inadequacy in equal measure. I felt as if my message was somehow inadequate by comparison, because I had to be grateful for not having experienced the traumas they describe, or because I was not doing the fantastic community work they were promoting.

However, the joy of being part of a supportive tribe is getting the skillset and encouragement to deal with and reject those negative feelings. If you are reading this, remember your message is as important as the next person's. We all have different needs.

I tried not to listen to news, but it does tend to gatecrash the party. The raging fires of the Black Lives Matter campaigns seemed to have cooled in the mainstream, but in sport was sorely tested, and I have to note the vociferous minority in sport and on social media did get my attention. The acts of those booing and trolling the young footballers who missed penalties in the Euro 2020 final will never cease to shock me.

I know without a shadow of doubt that life is so precious. We lost good people during this time (not necessarily to COVID) but were unable to pay our true and proper respects; this pandemic robbed us of our planned Christmas (that we didn't know would be the last) with Mummy A, as I fondly referred to my mother-in-law, and that bites.

3. Freedom: When Boris Johnson announced all legally enforceable restrictions would be removed on July 19, I was surprised by my level of vexation. "We are not ready," I said to anyone who would listen. The employers would take advantage, I wailed, not to mention people throwing caution to the wind.

It seemed I wanted to have my cake and eat it. I know I cannot live all life from my house, so I just had to work out in my head why I was vexed. Yes, I liked being in my house, but it's not as if I was not going out; I was already going to tae kwon do, but I did not go back to the gym until the end of July. I wondered if I had become like Pavlov's dogs, and the cue to leave the house was only to go to the shops and to take or collect shopping from my friend.

So, to answer the question. Have I progressed? It's a resounding yes. I have graduated from my two-ingredient bread to fully kneaded, water, flour and yeast bread. I have been privileged and honoured to have presented workshops at the recovery college and other places. As working from home quickly became the norm, I settled into my routines and passions with joy: cooking, baking, filming and presenting, all with the desire to choose happiness, encourage others and, with gratitude, the love of God and all my family.

Nike Akiti

C all me a happiness champ on a mission to help people always choose health and happiness, by beating faddy diet blues and practising self-care and love. My name is Nike Akiti, aka msnikkidee. Curious? Good. Read on to see what makes me, well ... me.

Nowadays, I hail from Luton, a child of Nigerian parents, wife, sister, friend. I love people, but not the naysayers. I want to go everywhere, and I still wish I had met Nelson Mandela. I am scared of not making a difference but am trying to show people it's never too late to follow their dreams. I am determined the world will be a happier place. I value freedom, good health and good relationships. I'm still proud of becoming a black belt in tae kwon do and now I'm proud to be a co-author, but still my bio is a work in progress!

Chapter 16.
Finding Myself and New Passion
Letitia Lorraine Thomas

My disability is a part of me. It isn't who I am and doesn't mean that I can't live my life.

My disability doesn't stop me from being myself. It is my friend, not my enemy.

Love me and my disability. My disability doesn't mean I haven't got a brain or feelings, or stop me being a loving, caring, friendly person.

Don't judge me because you see my disability. I don't let my disability rule me: I rule my disability.

9/7/20

I had a little chat with Junior Giscombe. He sent me a video of him performing other old skool singers and he has done a few things for my dad due to me. I had a great workout and conversation with Sacha yesterday and yes, Rita, he might be able to talk when I do my session in January. I have been journaling and watching some things on Netflix. I have been getting to know Sherell better and I'm sure that we're going to be good friends forever. I haven't done any Christmas shopping this year and it definitely feels weird. It has been a weird week on the dating app, but I'm still enjoying the journey to finding love. I was asked by my best friend's mum if I'm going to have a vaccine and I was really honest with her and said if I have to, I will, but I'm really unsure about it. This tier-three stuff just before Christmas is totally bull, if you ask me, and they wonder why some people are so annoyed with the government. I'm so shocked by the sad news about Mark Clarke. He has done so much for the community and it was fantastic to get to know him and be around him. Until the next time, stay safe and keep following your dreams no matter what.

17/12/20

Hello everyone. Life has been good. I have written a poem for Wayne Pilgrim, who is a hairdresser and photographer and a DJ, a family friend. I had yummy jerk pasta made by Jade and I can't wait for her to make it again. I am planning to have one of my best friends come and stay for a weekend once I have changed care agency. I had a great workout and conversation with Sacha today. I'm really looking forward to the next mosaic workshop, which is tomorrow afternoon. I have been listening to music every day and I'm really looking forward to seeing JLS in Birmingham in November. It is my first concert in years and I'm going with my cousin, Michaela, and my dad is driving us there and back, but he's not coming inside, lol. Until the next time, stay safe and keep following your dreams no matter what.

9/6/21

Summertime

It's summertime and the sun is out and shining bright. We can wear our summer clothes. It is hot and we feel the heat, so we get our legs out because it's summertime. We enjoy the sun. We sit in the garden because it's summertime. Summertime we go on holidays in the sun. Summertime we enjoy pool parties and barbecues with family and friends. Summertime means we can do outdoor festivities and enjoy the fresh air. Summertime is when we get a tan and eat ice cream.

17/6/21

Life

Life is all about loving yourself and others. Life is all about embracing yourself and the uniqueness of others. No matter what, life takes you on a journey.

Life is like a roller coaster ride: you have your ups and downs in life. Your experiences in life can make you stronger and wiser.

Life can be full of surprises and adventures. Life can be fun and enjoyable, life can be tough, but you will always get through it.

In life you make friends. In life you meet new people and find love. In life you might get your heart broken and fall out with someone. In life you make mistakes and learn from them.

In your life you will figure out your soul purpose and change someone else's life.

24/6/21

In my world I am who I am. I am no different from anybody else in my world and I have the same thoughts and feelings. Some days are better than others in my world.

I have good and bad experiences in my world. I have good and bad, negative people in my world. I have good and bad influences in my world. I have my own thoughts and opinions in my world. I have disagreements in my world.

In my world nobody is perfect, not even me in my world. Some people think that I have no understanding or can't speak because of my cerebral palsy. In my world, I laugh, I cry. In my world, I like, I dislike.

I have a great family in my world, and I have great friends in my world. I love creating things. I love having fun in my world. I dream about my future in my world. I appreciate everything that I have in my world.

19/8/21

After being in lockdown for nearly two years, I can honestly say that I have learnt a lot about myself and others who are in my life. I have learnt to put my mental health first and take time out for myself; self-love is very important. I started to write poetry during the lockdown and it has truly helped to clear my head. If I am having a tough day, it makes me feel better. I always try to tell myself, every day, I am a tough, strong, independent woman who can do anything even though some days I don't feel like I am. I am so glad that we have technology and music because it has kept me connected with my family and friends, and kept me sane during this uncertain time. Now that everywhere is starting to open up again and I am double-jabbed, I have started to go around to my nana's house every other Thursday, like before coronavirus came. I have been to a few gatherings. I recently got the role of web volunteer for the disability resource centre and I am reporting on the 2020

Paralympics. I love volunteering at the disability resource centre.

1/09/21

Letitia Lorraine Thomas

I am Letitia Lorraine Thomas, but people call me Tishy. I am thirty-five years old. I was born with a disability called cerebral palsy, which affects my arms, legs and speech. I went to Lady Zia Wernher School in Luton.

At the age of two until I was eleven, I had a few operations on my feet. From age eleven, I went to Ridgeway School in Kempston. When I was fifteen, I had surgery to straighten my spine. I left Ridgeway School a year early, to go to Hereward Residential

College in Coventry. I was there for three years and the subject I took was GCSE drama.

I am a volunteer at the disability resource centre, the co-author of two books, creative director for Verelba, part of the Simply Deez team and the Pamtengo Radio social media team. I'm also a poet.

Chapter 17.
My Strength, Faith and Determination Within One Year Later
Stephanie Powell

A lot was still changing in my county and in my home too. Lockdown is still happening ...

I had endured many changes within the home because of this. My health was still under assessment and I was still waiting on answers. There had been many delays because of the changes in the health system and in the world. I was dealing with appointments that were now being done through video calls and phone consultations. Face to face was becoming more difficult because of COVID.

What happens to those who don't understand technology, and particularly the elderly or those who choose not to do things in this way?

I waited patiently with little explanation of what I had been experiencing. It has been a real waiting game. To help myself, I read book upon book and used other research materials and any knowledge I had to get some clearer answers. This filled my time, although I should have been taking things easy.

There were many moments I felt at a loss, or real despair, exhausted with feelings of excruciating physical pain and emotions of all kinds on top of that, with long, waking hours of trying to get though the day. This wasn't easy to accept and still today isn't what I'm used to.

I felt numb and overwhelmed with what I was hearing and not knowing what my life may now hold. I felt low in the winter months, wanting to get on with life and work towards goals I had planned.

Now I have an invisible disability taking hold of me. I never thought this would be me. I am now learning to fight through it. There are days it really isn't easy.

I will keep fighting and do whatever is in my power to get my life back on track, with self-motivation and determination. But now I need a helping hand too. I hope it's only temporary, because I will carry on doing the things I want to do. I still feel I have so much to offer, but I may have to do things in a different way.

Dealing with people who can be quite judgemental really doesn't help. How would it leave you feeling if it was done to you? So have a heart with the things you say, and think before you speak.

I have always watched and admired those with a disability who also find determination and don't seem to give up or let things get in the way. As the saying goes, where there is a will there is a way. I will get there. And, I hope, so too will all those suffering from COVID who are still fighting for life. No one knows what the future now holds.

What Helped Through Lockdown!

Birth of *Life Inna Lockdown 2020* from weekly Zooms
The love of so many good people that I could turn to
Family, good friends, old and new, neighbours too
Motivation, strength, determination and faith
Lockdown has contributed to some emotions and pain.

Seeing each morning and blessed to still have life
Although not always perfect to start fresh again, new
Changes after changes! Numb from sad news too
Health up and down like the point of a compass
Reality that made me think! Sit back and reflect …

What is really important right now for me in my life?

I am grateful for those that have supported me in my most difficult times. Lockdown will be one of those experiences that will never be forgotten. In my home alone, we have experienced many changes and much sadness along the way.

The love of those around us and the support we try to give each other reinforces the love and bond we have for each other that was lost at times.

We may all have had our ups and downs, but just keep checking on each other.

The hardest part is not seeing family or friends face to face for so long because of circumstances and distance and being able to do things or go out without thinking, "Oh, I need a mask." Also, the need to keep my distance when able to get outside with assistance. I was still feeling unease at times when out, but this is slowly passing.

Missed opportunities

Watching young family members' years of important development. The visits and memories we usually share together I will never get back.

Meeting with friends face to face has been missed. That could have made a difference if things were not this way.

Unable to get out because of how I feel. Battling by the second, minute or hour in different ways. Lack of sleep contributed in how my days panned out.

Previously booked plans halted. Birthdays, Christmas couldn't be celebrated in the way I would choose.

Looking back

I thought I hadn't achieved much during lockdown. But really, I have accomplished a lot.

Weekly Zooms and workshops of interest.

A few walks in the park with my husband, who has given so much support.

Putting things in place to help myself.

New hobbies. Well-being and self-care.

Overwhelmed, it's the first anniversary, with a face-to-face meeting with some of my co-authors from book one.

Future

My beliefs now are more aligned with the universe, faith, hopes and my dreams.

Staying positive is what I am trying to do again, to get my life back on track. It may be slow and hard sometimes, but I know I will get there, slowly but surely in my own way with my intuition, love, support and God's guidance!

Stephanie Powell

I always aim to be optimistic, with a positive outlook and with a caring soul throughout life. I am a loving wife, mother, motivator to myself, family, friends and others.

For many decades, I have worked with passion and purpose to support and shape the future of children with their families as a nursery keyworker and teaching assistant in educational and social sectors through encouraging and enhancing their development.

My interests are reading, poetry writing and creativeness. Nutritional healthcare and well-being has also been a passion that I have been pursuing, starting with my own wellness, with the hope of helping others in the near future.

I know, through my own life experiences, that without health there will be no life. Relaxing with family and friends brings me fun, laughter, happiness and pleasure.

This is my third written piece in collaboration with others, with a view to producing my own in the near future.

Chapter 18.
There Are Butterflies in My Garden
Helen Garrand

Never in my wildest dreams did I think the lessons I learnt from the first lockdown and my garden would give me the strength and courage to deal with the two other lockdowns which were to come.

By September 2020, my garden had become a focal point for passers-by to look at and enjoy with all its colours and smells, having been born out of lockdown. It symbolised the emergence of the butterfly from within.

During the autumn and early winter, things around me in the world were certainly out of control. Should we or shouldn't we lock down? The only control I had was over my garden. I had the power to help plants survive over winter and the power to bring new life into the world from seed and bulb.

I suddenly realised how much you can learn from gardening and relate to your own life. When I was busy planting the strawberry runners to grow new plants for next year, I had my first glimpse. Using old soil in the bottom of the plant pots, I had to sift through and remove much of the dead roots and rubbish. This I had to do so that new roots could be established. When I thought about this in relation to myself, I realised how clearing yourself of negative thoughts from the past can help you to build positive roots for the future. Filling the remainder of the pot with new compost full of nutrients would again enhance growth. Filling your own life with positive thoughts will make you grow stronger.

It was February 2021 and, yes, we were still in lockdown for the third time. I decided that I would use this time to create new life by planting seeds. My living room became an indoor greenhouse. As it was my first time planting seeds, I was fascinated at the differences in how each seed was to be grown; having to plant at the correct depth with the correct soil, with some put into propagators and others grown in the dark. This made me think about how during lockdown you had the time to think of all the things that make you happy; your dreams which you could use to make positive changes, whether it be with relationships or a career move. How could we prepare ourselves to truly grow?

After just a few days, sometimes a week, there appeared new growth and each day, with plenty of watering, warmth and light, the plants grew stronger. In our lives, we too need nurturing. Our 'water' is a flow of positive thoughts, comments and experiences surrounded by the warmth of loving family and friends to give support when needed. Having time to think of what obstacles could hold you back from achieving your goals provided us with a guiding light for our individual journeys of discovery and growth.

Once the seedlings had grown big enough, the time came when they needed to be moved into a bigger pot, as the roots had reached the bottom of the pot and could grow no more, threatening the plants' continued growth. Lockdown gave us time to consider how our own roots were growing and look at ways we could perhaps move to bigger pots to expand. Perhaps, by taking up a new hobby, doing a course and gaining new skills, our bigger pot may be that dream job with more prospects.

And so comes the time when the plant needs to be introduced to the great outdoors, which is soon to become its forever home. Spending only a little time to start off with building up time each day hardens the plant to any conditions it may encounter. Emerging after lockdown and the lifting of restrictions can be viewed in the same way. For some, being allowed to mix and go out again has seemed very daunting and fearful. However, others have seen it in a more positive way – a way to get back to normal a life where we would have to harden ourselves to the realisation COVID is here to stay and we have to learn to live with it to survive.

It is June 2021 and lockdown has been over for three months now and my garden is growing in colour. The strawberries are giving of their fruit, which can be seen as a present to thank both God and the human who has nurtured it to this point. Our fruits of lockdown can be seen in the getting together of friends and families again and being able to hug after so many months of not being able to.

July comes and the plants are very well established. The sunflowers are blooming and the colours and smells are once again alive. People passing by are again enjoying looking in and saying "wow". There are still a few things left to do in the garden but they will get done. The garden, me and society have once again survived the perils of COVID. There are again butterflies in my garden, but they are free to fly wherever they want, as are we.

Helen Garrand

I am a volunteer at my local PDSA charity shop. My joy is my garden, and I am grateful lockdown gave me the opportunity to develop this fantastic hobby. I have a love of digital creativity, producing photo collages, and helped to design and produce this year's *Life Inna Lockdown* calendar. I am very community orientated and get involved in projects and run events. Making people smile while they are having fun is my aim in life and I will do anything within my power to make this happen.

I have a BA (Hons) degree in psychology/sociology and a nursing background. Though I struggle at times with my health, I always try to stay positive and think of all the things I can do for others.

Chapter 19.
Pain to Purpose
Justar Misdemeanor

My name is Justina; however, I tend to use my artist name: Justar Misdemeanor. I use this pseudonym as I love to play with words and it also reflects my style of art and character. I like to push boundaries and be a bit controversial or provocative in my artwork while being a sensitive soul with a big heart that wants to fix the world.

Unfortunately, I've begun to realise I can't fix the world, but I can help some people in the world, even just for a minute. This realisation only came about more recently ... Lockdown has been a turbulent time for me to say the least, and a headache at the best of times. There was no energy to even look for the light at the end of the tunnel, let alone believe there could be one. After being a recluse for three years prior to lockdown, I was sure I could handle it better than most people, as I already endured my own lockdown for so long.

On the cusp of lockdown, I had operations on my breast, leaving me feeling less like a woman and temporarily out of work until eventually losing my job. At the same time, my then boyfriend was put in prison for breaking his probation and being violent towards me. Also, the strongest woman I've ever known was put into a care home: my grandma was broken too. It made more sense that the world was broken rather than my one and only grandma was broken.

I couldn't fix anything or anybody, which consequently broke me too. I had just started to rebuild some sort of life; leaving the house, being in a relationship and working, etc, only to have it all taken away in an instant!

So, once again, I retreated to my safe place, not wanting to be seen making myself even more isolated so no one would know just how much I was struggling. After several months, I began using some of the mental health services available online, eventually joining some Zooms, which helped me feel less alone, even just for a minute, in between the battle in my brain. Some days I don't know whether to sit down or stand up; that's how conflicted the war is between my depression, PTSD and anxiety. There is no comfortable or content place.

Trying to fight my demons, I joined a Simple Well event on the recovery college, which led me to discover the *Life Inna Lockdown* crew. They are beautiful, pure souls who instantly took me under their wing and showed me love can come from anyone, despite genes or blood ties, and they became my family almost immediately.

Virtually connecting with such a diverse range of amazing, interesting and loving people really changed my life. I probably would not have crossed paths with them if it wasn't for the virtual life that many of us have adapted to due to the lockdown.

Not long after meeting my new family, I was asked to be on an International Women's Day online event to share my story and artwork. I had the instant reaction of 'What, me? Why?' Obviously, nerves followed, but I conquered my fears and bravely told my story. I took the power and control of what happened to me rather than being ashamed and scared for people to know.

Before that day, I was adamant not to share my story, because I was too ashamed, embarrassed and scared, like I had done something wrong. Obviously, I know this is not the truth, and anyone else who feels like this, I understand how difficult these emotions can be to deal with. It was not your fault and you are not to blame. This is still a difficult sentence for me and hard for me to fully accept. I am starting to learn it can take an eternity to heal these mental wounds; however, turning my pain into purpose has helped me keep my head above water.

The weight that was lifted from taking the power and sharing my story on International Women's Day is beyond words. I was not judged, nor looked down upon or made to feel any less than I should. It empowered me and motivated me more than I could have imagined and, since that day, my life has snowballed in the most positive, productive way. I now participate in numerous online events for different organisations; talking about my life, mental health and art. I have also been running my own events to inspire creativity and encourage people of all ages to express themselves in any and every way possible. Organising these events and being part of so many others has helped my own mental health and has given me a purpose to wake up every day. It's a purpose I never imagined I would have had if it were not for certain events that unfolded due to the lockdown.

Art has always been the most important, constant love I have had and it has helped me with my mental health over the years. It has enabled me to express myself when I couldn't speak out or when my words were not heard, which is why I am extremely passionate about what I do, as I feel some children, myself included, didn't always have a voice, so I want to encourage people to speak out in whatever form they can and take away the stigma of mental health in different cultures. Combining my love for art and desire to help other people deal with their own mental health may not have happened in this way if it were not for the lockdown.

Despite some of the hardships I have endured because of lockdown, it has also benefited me by making it possible to meet some truly talented, pure and creative people, empowering me to pursue passions and find my purpose.

I would not be able to write this chapter or even breathe another breath if it wasn't for a living angel who has always wrapped their wings of love around me. From the moment we met you loved me like your own, loved me more than I have ever felt and shown me beyond words how much you care for me. Having that love from nowhere for no reason has kept me looking for the light at the end of the tunnel. You always say I don't know how much I mean to you, but you don't know how much you mean to me! You kept me going when no one loved me, gave me hope when

I couldn't believe and always told me I was going to succeed and now I see. Tracey Whitmore – you saved my life more than once, and with your continued love I continue to soar.

Justar Misdemeanor

Justar Misdemeanor is a UK-born artist, completing an interactive arts degree at Manchester School of Art.

Justar's love of art stems from childhood and is a vital part of her life; allowing her to creatively express thoughts, feelings and concerns while raising awareness on controversial, traumatic, social and political issues.

Justar is an exhibiting artist and mental health advocate, organising online events to inspire creativity and mental health; speaking on several Zooms to support and spread awareness.

Instagram: @Justar_Misdemeanor_Artist

@Justarmisdeanor_Art

www.facebook.com/idoartinnit

Chapter 20.
Inna Meltdown
Gary Huskisson

Who needs a lockdown, when I am in permanent
meltdown
Pain is now my safe place
A place where the codeine cannot reach
Where my screams for help, fail to filter through the
vacuum
Home is where the stent is
Peace is the hands of an overworked paramedic
While my head wallows in a pity pit

I am living without mental security
The wrong colour, the wrong sex and the wrong
ability
Having bed and breakfast in the doorway of Marks &
Spencer's
Lying right there, contactless with all the homeless,
Every day I play out of my skin
Don't call me English, no pride in being any part
British,

Even as a European champion, I am a like a skeleton
noir woman
I never win

I consume stress, as part of my balanced diet,
Hypertension, diabetes and cardiac investigation are
my constant companions
Systemic racism, maternal instrumentations,
employment aggravations, sporting acquisitions,
female flirtations and indecisive politicians,
Factors, why I have sweaty palms and increasing
palpitations,
I wear a hi-vis, made-to-measure suicide vest,
An Icon in High Street Fashion, accessorised with a
matching face mask option
"In the new normal," issues related to mental health
are always trending,
my new default setting is set to suicidal.

Caring for my elderly mother has become the
epicentre of my mental disposition.
Constantly reminded that old black mothers have
limited compassion, when it comes to their son's
depression,
The phrase "It is the way they were brought up," is
meant to give me some understanding
I need the congestion in my head explaining

I want a break from being everyone's rock,
everyone's anchor,
Please can someone tell Wikipedia, despite it being a
trait of being a Cancer,
I have not got a waterproof shoulder

My mum is the unofficial Queen of St Vincent,
The beautiful island in the Windward Islands in the
Caribbean
Officially she is my mum; I wasn't there at the
conception,
After comparing slanting eyes,
M' dad seeing off the milk and postman with a
cutlass,
I can confidently say that I am her son, her only son
Even though there have been times, where she has
been in denial,
That she was even present at my birth,

She has given me canine hearing, so I can hear her
whining and bellowing,
"Garreee whe you gone wid all ya noise,
Cum here with wid all dat poetry ting,"
With de longest birch, she wud hunt me down,
swishing and swashing "Jesus, who put the devil
inside you, spitting and rhyming."

She is now 80 years young,

Older than the cobbled streets of Coronation Street
and Hilda Ogden
Older than Betty's hotpot, but she is sweet and spicy
like Dasheen and some Plantin,
My mum came to the mudder country at just nnnnn-
nineteen,
A teacher, a healer, came with a letter from the
Queen
Dear Evena, (Evie – I am the Queen of England, the
moderator of the Queen's English, my English)
My kingdom needs you here, to make them NHS bed,
to play cricket and help me learn patois from Megan

The Black sheep in the family is now COVID-19,
My mother, a woman who has had two jabs of the
vaccine,
Acts like Queen Latifah with an M16
Mum now wants to kick Boris up his oven ready
bum,
But for me to care for her 24/7,
I require many large glasses of strong rum

As the masks come off and the sanitisers have no
more refills
My skin is dry and my soul has no will
Yet caring for my mum has put me into isolation
Social distancing is the length of my patients

What do I do? I wouldn't know what to do, even if I
knew what to do.
When did a son become a primary carer?
When does a mother become a service user?
When did I give birth to a mother?
I can see the one who severed my umbilical cord,
trudge her way to landfill,
Being Gary is driving me mental,
I would be better off if I was white and called Nigel

I can remember when she was the age I am now
Which is not me being sentimental but fearful
I never wanted to be in charge of the remote control
Streaming live is Gary's all over the world being
sacrificial
While everyone still is watching black people die on
the News at 5
Sympathising by covering their eyes
They must know the revolution won't be televised,
It will be downloaded as a box set into their tainted
minds

Breaking news an unimaginable number have died
of COVID-19 today
The yellow strapline at the bottom of the news rolls
by with nothing more to say
We have become immune to the increasing
obituaries,

Everyone knows the John and Jane Doe family
While flowers shrivel at eye see you.
I go about my working day

Time for us to be safe in pain
We are still divided in so many ways,
Life will never be the same
As we blow out the final candle flame
Let us be the light
I am saying no to injustice and yes to fair play
Come to terms with being a caregiver, no room for an
imposter
I will nurture all those withering flowers
Be a beacon for kindness, a 21st century torchbearer
Turning the other cheek, compare dot.com the
likeness
Not letting my grieving stop me from believing
Living a life that is golden
I am a child of destiny with the same old pain,
I am a believer, armed with a torch, notebook and
pen.

I want to see 10 million epitaphs to say on the yellow
strapline
BREAKING NEWS: I have got a lot to say; read on to
the next chapter.
AMEN

Gary Huskisson

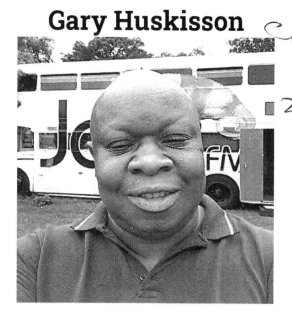

Gary Douglas Huskisson is straight out of The Fens, with ditches to the left and dykes to right. He's a trained storyteller, professional apple crumble eater, and a renowned, published poet intent on initiating change in the world by "Saying IT louder".

His mantra to life is (Proverbs 18:21): "The tongue has the power of life and death."

Here, in this written piece, he has served up lines from

previous poems between April 2021 and August 2021. As the masks come down, Gary says his unspoken words.

At the end of the day, he is still a little black fen boy all day and all night.

Chapter 21.
Mental Health Behind Closed Doors
Honei-May Stephenson-Dempsey

I'm starting this without a grin.

Where do I start? At the beginning?

Coronavirus tore me, like paper, in half.

Coronavirus stabbed and wounded me like a weapon, right through my heart.

My head started ringing – ding dong, ding dong – while I felt like my mind was a game of ping pong.

I felt like I was trapped, and that is not something to give yourself a pat on the back!

I saw the numbers of how many people had died. I felt absolutely sorry for all those people. I wanted to cry.

Feeling too weak to be the white dove and spread my wings and fly, fly way up high into the clear, calm but sometimes cloudy sky.

I missed shopping, theatre, restaurants and being with my friends. What the hell. When is this going to end?

Boris told us everything was closed. I lost my sunshine glow. All the doors, windows, and walls around me began to close; that's when I began to feel dark, glum, and low.

My anger wanted to scream, shout, blow, erupt like a ruby red, hot, scolding, scorching lava volcano, ready to explode, but that is not healthy. It's a BIG NO NO NO!

I should take deep breaths, that's what I know, and staying happy and positive will bring back my sunshine glow.

My happiness will make the plants and flowers blossom, bloom and grow.

I'm finishing this with a smile. This thing may take a little while, but with our hearts and happy minds, coronavirus you will take a dive!!

Honei-May Stephenson-Dempsey ©

Honei-May
Stephenson-Dempsey

I was diagnosed with autism, ADD and dyspraxia in 2009; however, it has never held me back from following my dream of acting and presenting. So I embarked on my journey of self-expression through creative arts to realise and achieve my dreams.

Known as the 'Rainbow Princess' to some, I love it when the rain and the sun come to form a beautiful arch. It brings hope and warms my heart.

The playful side of me is like a bit of comedy. I do 'stand up' for my friends and the laughter never ends.

I am grateful for this opportunity to express a different side of me, to embark on a new journey too with the *Life Inna Lockdown* crew.

Chapter 22.
Lockdown 2 – Time for Cultivation
Pamela E. Thompson

As I strolled through the valley of my mind
searching for answers to questions that
we're not mine, I began to cry, and I did not know the
reason WHY I thought all was
going well and suddenly I was feeling anxious,
unable breath and like I was walking
in hell!

From room to room I walked gasping for air as I tried
to talk, the people that I could
see were from my past, not present reality. This
dream it felt so REAL and the
negative energy I could feel, you want to walk back
into my life with all your baggage
and all your strife, time to let you go, time to weed out
my mind and grow.

Awaken from this slumber back in reality now it
would seem, I looked around and
asked myself what did this dream mean, what lesson
did I not learn that is causing
me concern in the burrows of my mind? I need to
introspect and find this trigger deep
within before I blow my top and you win.

So, my mind became my garden, my thoughts
became my seeds and I decided it
was my choice if I planted flowers or weeds. I began
to cultivate my mind day by day
and I kept what was needed and threw the negative
away. I began to pick sense out
of nonsense that was the new way for me because
not everything you say is relevant to me.

No time for mind clutter or your negativity; it's time
to lift this vibration and
change the frequency to elevate and empower the
true beauty of me.

So, I am breaking free from your chains of captivity;
it is time to face reality. Bound for
too long not able to see that you were still
captivating, distracting and trying to
destroy me. I have located the cutters and cut myself
free from your lies, derogatory

comments, and your victimisation of me.

No more unrealistic expectations will you have of me
as I now embrace the natural
energy of the mighty oak tree, restoring my strength
to overcome obstacles day by
day, I now live with the knowledge that everything is
going to be OK.
My morale will remain high like a Dove in flight in
the sky representing the peaceful
side of me that keeps me worry free.

No more guilt and condemnation, it is time to forgive
me, no more sabotaging the
blessings that the universe has sent me.

I will embrace the energy of the willow tree, the
structure, the strength, and the
stability to balance every part of me to withstand the
challenges placed in front of
me.

The willow is resilient and flexible, you see. It is all
about balance, learning, growth,
and harmony; that is the energy that I want to attract
to me.

In my mind I will embrace the pine tree both
feminine and masculine energy for
endurance, survival, and vitality for the continuation
of my peace of mind and
tranquillity.

But as I adapt within society I sense confusion,
stress, and anxiety amongst the
youngsters that are around me, so I urge you to
express your emotions that lead to
unrest. The anger, the judgements you hide just eat
you up inside, which progresses
to internal stress which builds up to mental distress
that causes worry, fear and
despair, thinking that no one really cares.

Search for the essence of who you truly are, find your
silver shadow, be that shining
star, don't buy worry, don't buy fear, turn to the ones
you trust and love and speak
your truth in their ear.

It's time to guide our life with positivity and
relinquish adverse company that drains
us physically, mentally, and emotionally, submitting
signals that are not very clear to
fit their agenda they hold so dear.

I am grateful for the blessings the universe sent to
me as I was born to be abundant,
I was born to be free; I was born to fulfil my life's
destiny.

Written by Pamela E. Thompson ©

Be Yourself everyone
else is taken.

Pamela E. Thompson

Stepping out of my comfort zone was one of the best decisions I ever made! On this lockdown journey there have been highs and lows; however, I am truly grateful for all I have experienced and learnt over this time, as I just took it one day at a time.

I have connected and met some beautiful, inspirational people and I am thankful that they made the choice to share their experience to elevate, lift and empower another.

Lockdown has allowed me to spend valuable time unravelling me to release what no longer serves me; my feelings of distress I have finally laid to rest.

Chapter 23.
Life inna lockdown I was feeling broke down. A black Queen without my crown.
Anna Rothery

Feeling like I was alone learning inner peace in my own home seeking simple things to fill my days trying to stay ahead of that grey haze.

Trying to keep my life real tight eating ice cream at midnight, learning to find peace with myself for once in my life me asking for help.

Solitary walks in the sunshine, praying for an end to lockdown, learning to accept doing nothing was OK, stripping all the BS away.

Dancing and singing like Beyoncé in the kitchen all day tapping into my inner child, making affirmations and doing things my way.

Turning loneliness into a superpower appreciating
every little thing in my life
101 songs to sing in the shower
Staring at my sisters on a laptop whilst tapping my
feet to hip hop.
We all found our way through doing what we had to
do. but one thing is clear in my mind

We couldn't have done it without our sister kind.

Anna Rothery

Anna Rothery became a councillor for the Princes Park ward in 2006 and was the only black Labour councillor in Liverpool for the first six years. She worked with Operation Black Vote nationally to ensure diverse representation. She went on to chair the Culture and Tourism Select Committee, Mayoral Lead for Equality and, latterly, became the first Lord Mayor of African Caribbean descent. She has been awarded a fellowship from Hope University for her years of service in community regeneration and economic equality.

SIMPLY DEEZ EVENTS

Making it happen ◆ *For you*

Sponsored by Simply Deez Events

www.simplydeezeventscic.com

Part funded by - Total WellBeing Luton

www.marciampublishinghouse.com

Printed in Great Britain
by Amazon